The Kitchen Sink Chronicles

by

Adele Cordner

First published 2021 by The Hedgehog Poetry Press

Published in the UK by
The Hedgehog Poetry Press
5, Coppack House
Churchill Avenue
Clevedon
BS21 6QW

www.hedgehogpress.co.uk

ISBN: 978-1-913499-51-8

9 8 7 6 5 4 3 2 1

A CIP Catalogue record for this book is available from the
British Library.

Begun during the outbreak of the Covid-19 pandemic in the UK in March 2020, this collection is a mother's perspective of the months that followed.

For Mum and Dad

Contents

PLEASURES PAST

12th March 2020

I hold out my arms.
My youngest jumps to me.
Our skins slide together
and droplets rise between us,
surprising our eyes
and raising our laughter.

Oh, the joy, the simple joy
of water, water,
all around us,
floating us together,
slowing our movements,
taking our weight
and letting us
fall into it,
making no more impression
on its surface
than a drop of rain
landing on a lake.

VIRAL SHOPPING

16th March 2020

It ricochets around the steel-beamed nave,
the small child's naive cough.
The man on his phone flinches for a moment,
turns his head, mid-sentence, calmly checks
his distance, then continues his mission,
worshipping in whispered tones.

In her blue gingham dress, the blonde girl,
hair dishevelled from nursery, flushed cheeks,
tugs at her sister as they fight over yogurt flavours
with the usual carelessness of youth.
I quicken my pace as she coughs again,
her mother too weary to seek out a tissue.

At every turn, expanses of cleared shelves.
Hard to remember what was here before
with all colour suddenly snatched away.
I read of the palest things: toilet tissue, chicken, soap, milk, flour,
whilst battered remnants of carrots, cabbages, swedes
lie jumbled for the taking in green plastic trays.

I pray I don't meet anyone I know. The need for conversation
is now too great, and how can we talk, two metres apart?
And how do we greet without any touch?
A supplicant now, I bow my head, lower eyes,
take short breaths beneath my scarf,
tighten my gloved grip on the trolley bar.

At least, I no longer need to explain;
self-isolating and social distancing our new vocabulary.
Just yesterday, stones were thrown at me:
hysterical, exaggerating, overprotective mother.
Easy ammunition for the privileged to aim,
for those who sip gin and place their bets.

We walk the last aisle, numb.
Process, orderly, in the pathway
of our fulfilment, our communion.
We will offer up our hard-earned treasure hoards,
turning slowly to ash, in return for our bread.
But here, at the altar, our life blood is drained.

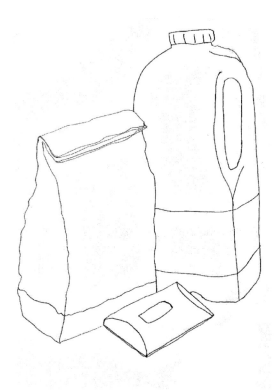

WATCHING THE NEWS

23rd March 2020

God help us all!
the Scotsman said
straight to camera lenses
focused on court steps,

cutting short his victory statement
with the bigger picture,
beads of sweat on his forehead
as he stepped away.

We wait, we sit on the sofa and wait,
sitting ducks, eyes on the clock,
a macabre appetite
for our own annihilation.

The virus maps across continents
in pretty pastel pixels.
Does a computer do the maths
or a human hand mark down each loss?

Bondi beach, covered in closely-packed crowds.
Sunbathers, swimmers, young, fit, tanned.
People think they are invincible,
that this world is theirs.

Prime Minister, grave, at his desk,
union flags colouring future history books,
but we know his bravado
will not turn this tide.

Firmness in his tone,
a recorded speech, measured.
Stay at home. Save lives.
Fines will be imposed.

Foreign words from his mouth;
We cannot cope. Not enough ventilators
to go round. Choices for the doctors.
He didn't write this one himself.

Nurses become our heroes now.
Retired, called back to join the front line
in a battle without weapons
that they never trained for.

IN THE ORCHARD

24th March 2020

Every tree, every branch is examined
for buds. Some more reluctant
to give me their pulse.

I stumble from one to another,
fingers tracing each stem,
any sign of life, a blessed relief.

One, two, three apple trees.
Last season's russets still wrinkled,
yet firm, in paper bags in the fridge.

Two plum trees show me pink
clenched fists. Six, seven, eight
pears, starting to green.

A lifetime ago, winter gone,
we poached them peeled in syrup,
cinnamon warming the room.

Pressed school shirts,
polished shoes and homework,
our trivial concerns back then.

Nine, ten, eleven; fine,
fluffy Bramleys, eldest boy's favourite,
in crumble, drowned in custard.

Twelve, thirteen, fourteen; dear
sweet eaters. Fifteen, fifteen, fifteen.
Frantic to find some sign of green.

Fragile twigs snap, brittle.
But you are not old, I tell the tree.
Last year, you bore the reddest fruit.

And see, the others still alive.
Same planting, same soil,
same shade, same sun!

I shake the trunk
so I might raise her up
like Turner's Oak at Kew.

Hands on her boughs,
I call back the old faith.
Make it stop. Give me life. Give me hope.

Tears streaming. Sixteen, seventeen,
eighteen; the last. White blossom open,
stamens welcoming bees.

DON'T TOUCH HER!

27th March 2020

The postman starts
at the yelp I make.

He backs away slowly
then darts through the gate.

I chastise the dog
and storm up the path.

She follows, tail down,
confused by my bark.

Fill the Belfast sink.
Squirt in her shampoo.

Don rubber gloves.
In she goes too.

Try to remember
which side was touched.

Left or right?
Was he wearing gloves?

I picture my son,
laid out last night,

flat on the sofa,
dog sprawled by his side.

In the hospital letter,
his appointment date.

In the bathroom cabinet,
his medicine sachets.

At once, I decide
on the safest course of action;

our loopy cockapoo
gets a full baptism.

COUNTDOWN

31st March 2020

Each day that passes by,
each hour, each minute, each tick
is another one alive.

I should sing to the stars,
dance with my children, my love,
but I am numbed by fear,

heart clenching at the slightest cough,
watching the clock like a thing possessed,
tick, tick, tick,

passing days and nights in isolation,
in fits of action and inaction,
in hope and hopelessness,

in knowledge and in ignorance
of the world that passes outside,
climbing the days to the mountain of fourteen,

my pen, my only staff, trailing ink
in pathetic attempts to drive
the dark shadow from my door.

AT THE CEMETERY

3rd April 2020

In memory of Ismail Mohamed Abdulwahab

Again, sun rises
on the undressed trees.
They stand to attention,
not a single twig moves
in respect for another soul
lost to the moon.

No family mourners
at this graveside
as the small coffin
greets the freshly-dug soil,
led by men in masks
wearing white, hooded suits.

No flowers.
No shroud.
No body embalmed.
No hymns.
No speeches.
No ceremony.

But a cradle
of wood
for all eternity.

LAMENT OF MOTHER EARTH

4th April 2020

Oh, my darlings, I did my best;

dyed deadly berries in the deepest shades,
added spots, stripes, spikes to forbidden leaves,
washed fungus with red, gave rattles to snakes,
a fin to the shark, slowed down sting rays,

wiped out great lizards and froze deep seas,
took other's food far from your reach,
grew forests too dense and rivers too long,
buried unsafe gases deep underground,

gifted some mammals with speed and flight,
armoured the animals you cannot eat
with scales, quills, shells, thick bristled skin,
a bitter taste or bony wings.

But still you persisted;

you trampled and climbed,
you chopped and scythed,

you dug and cut,
you tracked and shot,

you drilled and mined,
you dragged and drained,

you netted and trapped,
you killed and hacked.

You sold. You bought.
You ate. You caught.

A SHORTAGE OF LOO ROLL

6th April 2020

For my boys

I
The basics

After dinner, we discuss the shortage of loo roll.
We're down to four between five of us.
I do a quick calculation of the kitchen rolls.
I could tear them into squares, thin out the layers.
Only half a box of tissues.
Why didn't I buy more last week?
My eldest son avoids my eyes.
This isn't hard when he's over six foot and I'm just past five.
I call my mum. She has eight, for her and dad.
She offers to share but I can't bear
the thought of them going short and I'm reluctant to drive,
plagued by the dread of an accident,
an ambulance ride to our swamped A&E, already a national hotspot.
We'll manage somehow, I breeze,
warming my hands in the washing up water.
The dishwasher is broken.
No hope of a repair right now.
My thoughts run to fuel.
Did you check the pellet store?
I try to sound casual as I ask my husband.
He's out like a shot, and back, looking pale.
Did you place an order?
I thought you did.
Silence.
I'll email tomorrow.
Silence.

II
Sustenance

We check through the freezer.
Minced beef, sausages, smoked salmon from Christmas,
leftover curry in takeaway tubs.
We could last a month on all this.
In the pantry, no baked beans.
No ketchup!.
God. Three boys. No ketchup.
Husband googles home-made ketchup.
Sounds tasty, he says.
The boys roll their eyes in disgust.
I know it'll never happen.
No home delivery slots.
I sit up until midnight. On the stroke, I'm set up.
Phone and laptop. Two supermarkets.
Yes! I get one -
for three weeks time.
My hands are shaking as I shop.
Please Internet, don't cut out.
No bulk packs available.
Maximum, three of each item. Limit of 85.
Each banana counts as one. Delete the crisps.
No flour, eggs, baking powder.
But 13 pages of cakes, 18 of chocolate treats.
Where did we go wrong?
No loo roll, of course. Tissues. That'll do.
Checkout. Sit back. Breathe. I have a headache.
Close laptop. Turn off phone. Do not turn on the TV.
Take a short nightcap up to bed.
My eldest boy is leaving the bathroom.
He avoids my eyes again,
but now he's clutching his abdomen.
Can you call the doctor?, he says.
I have a flare up.

III
Help

Morning. I am checking my emails for a response
from his specialist nurse.
The doctors are too busy fighting fires.
He gives an appointment.
The unit has moved away from the heat.
My boy breathes more freely,
comforted by the distance
and the mask and gloves I hand him.
For the first time, he has to go it alone.
We make a plan for afterwards:
a strip down at the back door,
washing machine left open,
shower door ajar.
Husband packs the car with soapy water in tupperware,
a portable basin,
home from home,
and off he heads.
Thank god he filled the car with petrol last week.

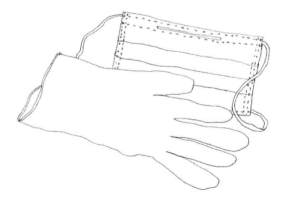

IV
Survival

For weeks, his meals consist of mashed potato
or rice, chicken or fish and carrots.
We don't like him to do it alone
so we all eat together,
facing the blandness with war-like stoicism.
The shopping arrives.
Oat milk. Check. Gluten-free bread. Check. Rice noodles. Check.
Dispose of all possible packaging, antibac the rest.
A replacement. Three kg bags of Essential carrots
replaced with one Organic.
I could scream.
Instead, I sit at the kitchen table and calmly
write a poem about loo roll on my phone.

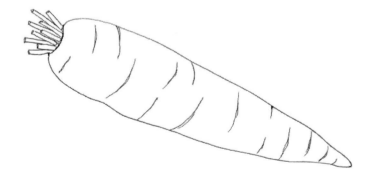

888

18th April 2020

Only a month ago
an Italian number
less than this
had shaken me
to my core.

Lost in 24
small hours.
Our tears
are never
enough.

Yet here,
today,
conditioned now,
this number
sends no shock.

In fact, I find myself
lifted
by a heart beat
of hope
amidst the pulling pain.

The number
has rolled back
from the hilltop
it steadily climbed
on solemn Easter days.

A sign
that maybe,
one day,
maybe,
life might be reclaimed.

ANOTHER FINE DAY?

20th April

Should sun still shine on this beleaguered land,
make blossom pink and white on cherry trees,
light curls of lambs, scent daisies to draw bees,
let gentle waves lap swathes of untouched sand?

Should wind not rage as humans battle on?
Should litter not be whipped through empty streets
and rain gush down from gutters while we weep
for all sick souls whose lives are not so long?

But sun has kept us calm through all the pain,
made us look up while storms might rage within.
So nature steadfastly has played her part.
She spares us from the deluge of spring rain
that we might step outdoors and there begin
to find a way towards a lighter heart.

SWALLOW CHICK

23rd April 2020
For my girl

I ache for my daughter through these lockdown days
wandering the garden, taking photos on my phone
of first daffs then rose buds to send to her,

when, suddenly, there she is, my swallow chick
perched high on the aerial, so proud to be home.
I'd recognise those bright eyes anywhere.

Last June, I found her helpless on the garage floor,
her nest a mess of soil and feathers around her,
her parents darting frantically about my head.

I was nervous, but I knew she needed me,
cupped her heart in my hands and placed her
gently in a tree, her elders shrieking all the while.

But, straightaway, she launched herself to the ground,
hopped around my feet, brave and unaware
of the lurking cats anticipating a snack.

I stored her safe in a shoe box while I built a little cot,
gathering leaves, petals, feathers from her nest,
then tucked her up high on a garage shelf.

But, in moments, she was out again, put back
again, and again, for days and days, until, at last,
from beam to beam, and out, she flew!

Now, she is back, sleek plumes, colours deepened,
tail feathers long and strong.
What was it like, Africa? I've never been.

As I take her photo, I imagine her there,
independent, exploring savannahs with her kind,
and the old, now familiar, ache returns.

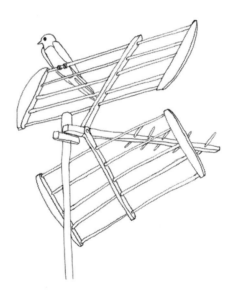

THE EMPTY SPACE

11th May 2020

In memory of Angela Platt, inspirational poet and leader

I didn't hear it fall. No wonder the dogs barked.
Such sensitive souls, warning us
that our world was under threat.

It only just missed the apple tree. I am in awe
of its size, lying prone. It seems at least twice
its upright height. I had no idea it would fall.

The leaves already droop, rootless. Just hours ago,
they homed birds, squirrels, spiders in lively foliage
freshly unfurled to blue skies.

It left behind its uppermost boughs, left them
hanging high, raggedly torn but balanced
in the limbs of its neighbour, swaying in calming wind.

There is an empty space where this Sycamore stood,
giving me a sight line through woodland, over hills,
almost as far as my parents' house.

ON PAUSE

29th May 2020

For a strong friend

Inside the clinic
in a test tube
in the freezer
her embryos wait.

Outside her front door
out on her street
no children play
no babies in prams.

One less stress to face
when she steps out
for her daily walk
with nothing to show.

In white light
between the shelves
a fertility technician
inspects the paused lives.

Patience, she whispers.
*Let the world cool down
before we make you warm.*

SPEECH BUBBLES

5th June 2020

Lockdown. Social Distancing.
Self Isolation. Shielding.
All now neatly filed with:
Stay Home. Save Lives
Save our NHS.

A Protective Bubble
is the shiny new addition
to our weaponry of words
in this quick-to-learn language
of pandemic survival.

If I had a superpower as a gift,
I truly wish I could magic this;
stronger than a shield,
safer than a cave,
comforting and comfortable,

a transparent, shiny, bouncy
bubble. Invisible to all
but me. Provided
it was big enough
for my whole family.

BREAKOUT

10th July 2020

It was the heather pink that hooked me,
drew me to admire the depth of colour
and subtle streaks of silver
woven through white stripes.

I had to have it. Hold it. Possess it.
After 114 days without stepping
into a single shop, the urge to pick it up
was too great. Not a thought of

who might have touched it,
who might have breathed or coughed
onto the surface that I now pressed
into my palm. I couldn't put it back now

could I? It was mine.

And then, something snapped.
In a wild hysteria,
I took another and another:
a beautiful white piece, colour of the moon,

another pink one, pale grey, this one
in charcoal, these two, soft stone,
until I was weighed down with it all,
could carry no more back to my cave

and facing the fact that my dirty hands
were stuffed in pockets packed with pebbles
that would need disinfecting, and, probably
I should wash my coat as well.

THE LONG VIEW

1st August 2020

For M

We are level with the birds.
Overhead, a flock sweeps black
before cruciferous white clouds,
backlit by an azure blue sky.

On the horizon, grass-quilted cliffs
drop straight to the green wash,
godly in their magnitude, renowned
for their well-aged creases.

Wind mingles high shrieks of children
and gulls as the sea takes prisoners
of surfing families, changes heart
and tosses them back to the sand.

Down the hill, queueing for fish & chips,
wetsuited strangers smile
at one another, talking softly,
touching within their groups.

On the bank, shadows pass.
A pair of corvids alights.
Eyeing me, they hop around, outing
worms, unafraid and unashamed.

THE SHAPE OF THINGS

14th August 2020

For a special friend

In a crystal sea, shapes of crimson
shift on the tide,
intricate spheres, perfectly symmetrical
patterns on repeat.

On TV, shapes in crimson
shift across headlines,
intricate spheres, perfectly symmetrical
patterns on repeat.

My hand is touched by the seaweed.
I lift it from the water.
It wilts to a slime,
draped across my fingers.

The virus invades the blood of my friend.
It drains her energy, burns her body,
gives her fitful sleep and pain
deep in her lungs.

I let the plant slip back to the sea.
It regains its natural form,
coral-like, gleaning nutrients
through fine fronds.

My friend isolates for weeks.
Her daughters leave food at her door.
At last, her body expels the alien cells.
They wilt, at last, to memory.

RESULTS DAY

20th August 2020
For my baby

The email arrives.
At first, I am stunned
then spinning with stars.

A photo for school
holding up his phone
hand around his future.

We bounce around the kitchen,
forget for a moment
that he's not at school

clutching his paper printout
in a huddle of friends,
embarrassed by the presence

of proud parents and teachers,
forget he missed his leavers prom,
his teen holiday, his summer term.

*

Later, a burger
with fries to celebrate,
oozing with ketchup.

Then, family film night.
Funny Girl. We watch as she
finds her place in the world.

WINDMILLS

28th August 2020

In memory of a precious aunt

At the mountain top, windmills
breathe deeply in a crisp sky,

sweeping up air and exhaling power
with each rotation of solid sails.

On this drive back from the far west coast,
I am struck by the sharp season change.

A low sun lights up trees turning
inward, shutting down already,

though not yet September, preserving
themselves for the winter ahead.

*

Last night, they switched off the machine
that filled my aunt's failing lungs.

Her daughter held her hand
as her last breath slipped away.

*

When I reach my home town,
the sun drops behind me.

In my mirrors, the familiar landscape stretches
silhouetted by an amber rose sky.

ACKNOWLEDGEMENTS

I am delighted to have collaborated with my daughter Florence who has provided the illustrations for the book. It has been wonderful to share a creative project when the pandemic has forced us to be physically separate.

I would like to thank my parents, my husband Michael and our four children for their constant support and encouragement of my writing, and also NaCOT and Newport Stanza poets for their workshopping feedback which gave me the confidence to believe in myself as a poet.

This is my first poetry collection and I hope it serves as a fitting record of this trying time. Thanks to Mark Davidson of Hedgehog Press for having faith in it.

Adele Cordner
December 2020

ABOUT FLORENCE CORDNER

Florence lives in a flat in Surrey with her boyfriend and around 100 houseplants. In her free time, she is either tending her plants, digging her allotment, or walking in the countryside. She draws inspiration for her art from the natural world, particularly British wildlife.

She specialises in embroidery, sketching and watercolour painting, and has been passionate about art her whole life. She will often sit on a video call with friends and sketch for hours at a time.

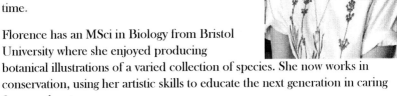

Florence has an MSci in Biology from Bristol University where she enjoyed producing botanical illustrations of a varied collection of species. She now works in conservation, using her artistic skills to educate the next generation in caring for our planet.

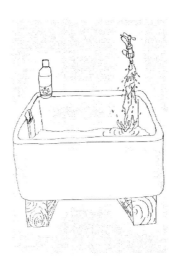

THOUGHTS ON THE KITCHEN SINK CHRONICLES

When I look back at the poems I wrote at the beginning of the pandemic, I see the immense shock that we all felt at the change of lifestyle, restriction of freedom and threat to our safety and health, particularly the threat to our loved ones.

I came to realise that these were things that we had taken for granted in most of our lifetimes, and feelings which most of us had been lucky never to experience before. I began to see the pandemic as a moment in time when all our lives and futures became forever changed, perhaps, in some ways, for the benefit of the planet as a whole.

I was fortunate to spend lockdown at home in rural South Wales during those difficult first months when the world seemed to stand still. The natural world around me, as always, was a constant comfort and salve.

Adele Cordner
December 2020